Park Perfect... Now!

John R. Wright, Jr.

John Wright, Drive Time, Inc.

Acknowledgements

Parallel parking is a skill that is used to evaluate whether or not new drivers are able to maneuver a vehicle especially while backing and turning. I developed this parking method because I observed many people making parallel parking much harder than it needs to be. This booklet is not intended to be a trick or Vu Doo magic. My intention is to help you learn what parallel parking is by finding reference points that are easy to understand.

A huge part of driving is did you look in the right place, did you communicate your intention to other drivers as well as did you control the vehicle. Mr. Tony Foderaro assisted in this effort by organizing the first 5 steps into a 1, 2, 3, 4, 5 order that is very easy to remember. We call it *"the 1-5"*. Tony is part of our team at Drive Time Driving School. Our team makes Parallel Parking easy for students every day. That's our job. We see what does work and what doesn't. I hope you will use *the 1-5*, because it will make your parallel parking learning experience better.

John R. Wright

Author, Park Perfect Now!
Owner, Drive Time, Inc.

John Wright, Drive Time, Inc.

Index	Page
Introduction	9
Parallel Parking Made Easy As 1-5	10-17
What Did I Do Wrong?	18
How Do I Fix It?	19
What Do I Do With These Stickers?	19
Sticker Placement	20
Stickers	21
Angle & Perpendicular Parking	23-25

The driver aligns cone A with the back tire.

Do the 1—5.

Step One

As the car pivots, look for cone B in the left side mirror.

Stop when you can see all of cone B and straighten wheels

Step Two

Step Three

Back straight until you can see the right rear tire about 12 inches from the white line.

The Driver will also be able to see cone A in the bottom right corner of the windshield.

Step Four

When the back tire is close enough to the curb, stop, turn the wheels all the way right and pull forward until the front tire touches the curb.

Introduction

My name is John Wright. I am the owner and lead instructor at Drive Time Driving School. It always amazes me how while everyone seems to have an opinion about parallel parking, most of the advice I've seen from parents and even *"so called"* experts is either not very helpful or even wrong. I see people struggle for hours trying to *"get it"* with no plan or any kind of solution that really works.

Parallel parking without a method is a lot like trying to solve a calculus problem, it can be confusing and even if you eventually do it right you're still not sure how you did it. Using Park Perfect Now will teach you how to Parallel Park quickly and easily and because you are using a step by step method to find specific reference points, you will know immediately if you mess up and how to fix it.

Practice is important, but, practicing something you don't understand is pointless and frustrating. Park Perfect Now will show you exactly how simple parallel parking really can be and will make your practice quicker and more effective. Park Perfect Now also gives you the tools you will need to successfully Parallel Park every time, both on the street and on a driving skills test.

First before I give you the step by step method let me make two things very clear:

1. **Practice:** Every skill you develop requires practice. Park Perfect Now will get you in the space with little or no practice, but, to be truly proficient you *will* have to practice. What's the difference then; everyone says you have to practice? Park Perfect Now will get you parking right away so you can spend time practicing parking not struggling without a plan.

2. **Use this Method Step By Step:** If you follow this method precisely, it will work precisely. If you deviate from the method than the method will not work as well. If you have difficulty you are probably forgetting a step if this happens, start over, go back to the method step by step and you will solve the problem.

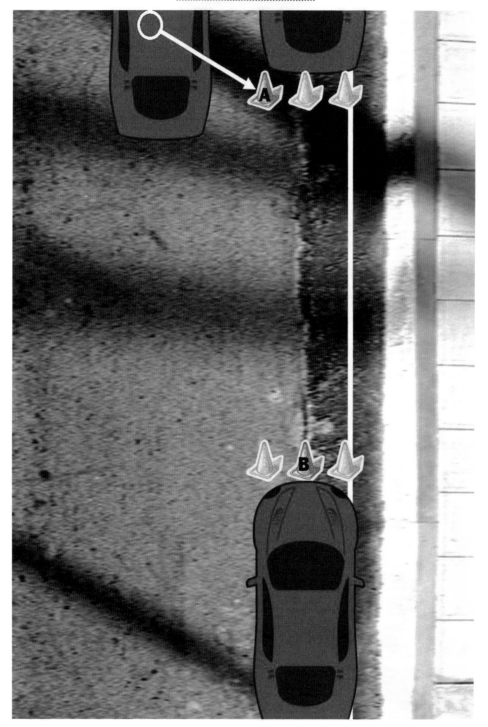

Park Perfect Now

Step one.

Align your back tire with Cone A (see page 6.)

You will see the Cone A in the rear passenger side window the Cone A should be all the way in the back of this window.

Now do the 1-5 (in). Count out loud as you do the 1-5.

1. Gear Selector (Reverse)
2. Signal the direction you are going (Usually Signal Right)
3. Turn the steering wheel (all the way) the same direction as you signaled.
4. Check all your mirrors to make sure your path is clear.
5. Check your blind spot. (especially over your left shoulder)

Tips:

One thing almost everyone agrees on is that for parallel parking the closer you get to the cones the better.

The 1 – 5 is very important to build the habit of making visual checks before pulling in or out of the space. Years of experience have taught me that if you count 1 – 5 as you do the steps you will remember them. If you don't count, you will forget the steps and lose points or even fail your parallel parking test. So don't risk it, while you are practicing say, "One" as you put the car in reverse, "Two" as you signal to the right, "Three" as you turn the wheel all the way right, "Four" as you check your mirrors, "Five" as you turn your head and check your blind spot. You may feel silly counting out loud at first, but, you won't feel silly *at all* when you pass your driving test.

On The Street:

You want to see the back corner of the car beside you in the back of the rear passenger window.

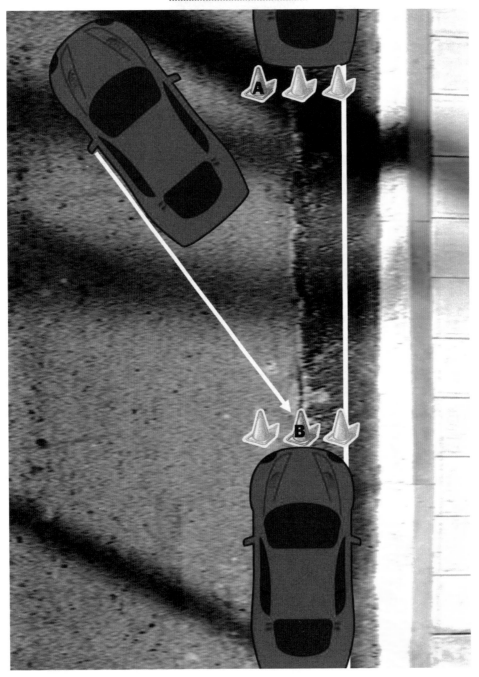

Step two.

Back up until you see the middle cone in the driver's side mirror. (see page 8.) Stop completely and straighten the wheel.

Tips:

It is ok to see a little of the third cone, but, you don't want to see all of the third cone in the driver's side mirror.

On The Street:

The middle cone is like the license plate of the car you are parking behind. So if you are parking on the street look for the license plate instead of the cone.

John Wright, Drive Time, Inc.

Step three.

Turn your right side mirror down and then all the way left. You should now be able to see your right side rear tire. Back up straight until you can see the curb in your right side mirror. Once you see the curb, get the back tire about 24 inches from the curb. (see page 10.) (On most driving tests there is a white line painted 12 inches from the curb. If you get your right rear tire close to the line you will be aligned perfectly.)

Once your back tire is close to the line, STOP, turn the wheel all the way left.

In order to make a legal park both right side tires should be within 12 inches of the curb. Continue backing up until your right side rear tire is close to the curb, but, be careful to stop before hitting a cone behind you.

Tips:

Make quick glances from the rear view and right side view mirrors. Check the space between the car and the curb and between the car and the cones behind you.

On The Street:

It is often difficult to judge distance between your bumper and the bumper of the car behind you, so be careful as you continue backing up.

John Wright, Drive Time, Inc.

Step four.

Turn the wheel all the way right and pull forward until the front tire touches the curb. Put the car in park.

On The Street:

Myth: some people teach that you must straighten the wheel before leaving your car. Fact: your car is more secure with the wheel turned right and front tire touching the curb. That being said: don't forget to check the spacing in front of and behind your car. Your car should be in the middle of the space to avoid being trapped by another driver.

Step five. (Exiting the Parking Space)

Put the car in reverse. With the wheels still turned right, back up. This gives you an easier angle to exit. Stop, now do the 1-5 (out). Count out loud as you do the 1-5.

1. Gear Selector (drive)
2. Signal the direction you are going (Usually Signal left)
3. Turn the steering wheel (all the way) the same direction as you signaled.
4. Check all your mirrors to make sure your path is clear.
5. Check your blind spot. (especially over your left shoulder)

Gradually exit the space while checking two areas: the blind spot over your left shoulder and the front corner of your car.

Summary:

1. See cone A in the rear passenger window, stop, do the 1-5.
2. See cone B in the left side mirror, straighten the wheels and continue backing up.
3. Check your right mirror (turn it down so you can see the curb and your tire), when the tire is 24" from the curb, turn the wheel all the way left and continue backing up.
4. Continue looking in the right side mirror, stop when the back tire is about 6 inches from the curb, turn the wheels all the way right and ease the front tire onto the curb, secure the car.
5. To exit: back up slightly with the wheel still turned right and do the 1-5 out and gradually straighten the wheels as you exit the parking space.

What Did I Do Wrong?

There are just four primary mistakes people make when parallel parking.

1. **You did not get close enough when you pulled up.** We discussed this already. Starting too far away from your destination makes it harder. If you were going to throw a soda can in the trash, would you walk over right next to the trash can or would you toss it from 10 feet away? If you said toss it, *bravo!* you are a risk taker you may never learn to parallel park very well, but, you are sure to have an exciting life. If you said get very close to the trash can and drop it in you may not have as much fun as some do, but, you are much more likely to be successful and you have already know the first secret of parallel parking.
2. **You did not start parallel to the curb.** Parallel parking is called parallel for a reason. You drive parallel to the curb. You park parallel to the curb. You should start your park with your car parallel to the curb and in order to park legally you will finish your park with your car parallel to the curb.
3. **I did not get within 12" of the curb.** Some people recommend pulling out of the space and starting over. I think this depends on how far from the curb you are: ie. If you are still 3-4 ft from the curb, sure, pull out and start over. But, if you are close but not close enough just wiggle it over. For detailed explanation of how go to **How Do I Fix It?**
4. **Oops, you forgot a step. No problem just pull out, review the steps and start again.**
   a. A very common mistake is to forget to look and stop for the middle cone in the driver's side mirror. If this happens just stop (DON'T TURN THE WHEEL AT ALL) Pull forward until you can't see the third cone (but <u>do</u> see the middle cone).
   b. Another common mistake is to forget to stop 24" from the curb. In this case the driver comes all the way back and touches the curb. In this case, simply turn all the way right and continue your park. Watch your right side back tire and stop before your tire crosses the line. Turn all the way left and back up until you are parallel to or touching the curb. If the back tire touches the curb, turn back to the right and pull forward if you are parallel to the curb congratulations you are done. Now pull out and practice more until you can remember the steps.

How do I fix it?

The best advice for learning parallel parking is to practice the wiggle move. The *"Wiggle Move"* is basically a mini-parallel park. The Wiggle move is what you would do if you needed to move a little closer to the curb, but, did not want to pull out of the space and redo the park. Turn your right mirror down to see the space between your back tire and the curb.

1. **Pull as far forward as you can.**
2. **Turn all the way right and put the car in reverse**
3. **Back up about half of the available distance and stop**
4. **Turn the wheel all the way left**
5. **Continue backing up**
6. **Repeat as often as necessary**

What about these stickers?

The stickers on the page 21 can be cut out and taped on the vehicle windows to remind you of the reference points. Place step one at the back of the rear passenger window. Place step two at the back of the front passenger window. Place step three at the bottom right side corner of your windshield. Place step four wherever you like.

The 1-5 and the stickers put the *now!* in ParkPerfectNow!. Place these stickers properly and you will instantly be miles ahead in your parallel parking practice.

Placement of the stickers

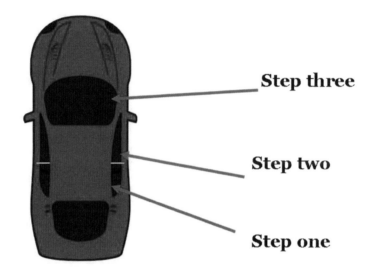

Step three

Step two

Step one

Step 1  HERE

DO THE 1 – 5

SIGNAL RIGHT, WHEELS RIGHT

BACK UP SLOWLY

Step 2 STOP Here

CHECK DRIVER SIDE MIRROR

FOR THE MIDDLE CONE

STRAIGHTEN WHEELS

BACK SLOWLY

Step 3 STOP Here

CHECK RIGHT SIDE MIRROR

BACK TIRE SHOULD BE

24" FROM CURB

TURN LEFT, BACK SLOWLY

Step 4 STOP

BEFORE TIRE HITS CURB

TURN THE WHEEL ALL THE

WAY RIGHT & PULL FORWARD

Cut out arrows and tape to windows according to the diagram on page 20.

John Wright, Drive Time, Inc.

Entering Perpendicular And Angle Parking Spaces

The most common mistake people make in perpendicular and angle parking is not moving far enough left to park on the right or not moving far enough right to park on the left. The more space you give yourself the easier your park will be. With this in mind remember the following five step process:

1. Stop with your head aligned with the middle of the space next to the one in which you want to park, turn the wheels all the way in the direction of that space.
2. Signal in the direction of the space you want to enter
3. Check your mirrors
4. Check your Blind spots
5. Straighten the wheel gradually as you enter the space.

Exiting Perpendicular And Angle Parking Spaces

The most common mistake on exiting has to do with looking around and backing slowly with wheels straight until your dashboard is even with the bumper of the car next to you.

1. With foot firmly on the brake select the proper gear
2. Signal the direction you want the back of the car to go
3. Check mirrors
4. Check blind spots
5. Back slowly until the dashboard or windshield is even with the bumper of the car next to you.
6. Steer in the same direction as you are signaling and continue out of the space, continue looking for hazards

Perpendicular Parking

First you need 10' of space between your car and the car next to you. Then line up your head with the middle of the space next to the space you are pulling into. Signal, turn the wheels all the way right, check your blind spot and mirrors before moving, and straighten the wheels gradually as you enter the space.

Angle Parking

First you need 4—6 feet of space between your car and the car you are parking next to. Then you need to see down the line of the parking space you are pulling into. Gradually steer into the space. Try to center the car in the space.

© Drive Time, Inc.

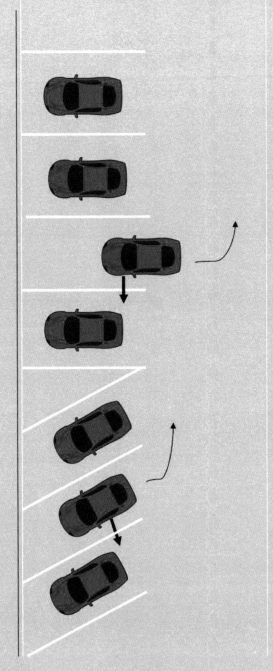

Exiting a Perpendicular Parking Space

Signal the direction the back of the car is going to go. Check in all directions and back slowly. Back up straight until you align the dashboard with the bumper of the car on your left if you are backing to the right (check right if backing to the left). Steer sharply as you exit the space.

Exiting an Angle Parking Space

Signal the direction the back of the car is going to go. Check in all directions and back slowly. Back up straight until you align your head with the bumper of the car on your left if you are backing to the right (check right if backing to the left) Steer sharply as you exit the space.

© Drive Time, Inc.

John Wright, Drive Time, Inc.

Please check out our website at 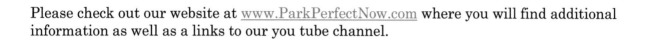www.ParkPerfectNow.com where you will find additional information as well as a links to our you tube channel.

Thank you for reading ParkPerfectNow!   I sincerely hope you find ParkPerfectNow! helpful in your driving learning experience. Good Luck and Drive Safely.

My name is **John Wright.** I am the owner and instructor at Drive Time Driving School. I started Drive Time because I love driving. I created Park Perfect Now! Because I found that 65% of teens have a near pathological fear of parallel parking. In fact, most of my students are more concerned about parallel parking than are concerned about being safe on the highway. So I learned very quickly that teens were more able to focus on my concerns about safety, if I could dispel their fears of parallel parking. Thus was born Park Perfect Now!

During my career in sales and prior to that in the Navy I had so much opportunity to drive, I now have more than 2 million miles of driving experience. This experience has given me a lot of insight into driving's, "best practices". I started Drive Time so I would have the opportunity to share this insight with new drivers. I also wanted a career that would allow me to be a positive role model to young people.

I am a christian husband and father of 3. I attend "Crosspointe Church of the Nazarene" on Nanticoke Rd. in Salisbury, MD.

I am a Maryland MVA Certified Driving Instructor, a Maryland MVA Certified Driver Improvement Instructor, a certified MVA classroom instructor, behind the wheel instructor, driver improvement program instructor and young driver improvement program instructor. I developed and gained approval from the MVA to use my own young driver improvement program, which I call "Protect Your Privilege". Drive Time is presently one of just four schools in Maryland approved to offer this program. I have attended West Virginia University, Anne Arundel Community College, Naval Nuclear Field Electronics Tech "A" School, and Nuclear Power School NTC Orlando.

12409801R10017

Made in the USA
San Bernardino, CA
20 June 2014